Abraham
Rodriguez

Reborn

central
avenue
POETRY

2024

Published by Central Avenue Poetry, an imprint of Central Avenue Marketing Ltd.
www.centralavenuepublishing.com

REBORN

Trade Paper: 978-1-77168-371-5
Ebook: 978-1-77168-372-2

Published in Canada
Printed in United States of America

1. POETRY / LGBT   2. POETRY / Subjects & Themes - Inspirational

1 3 5 7 9 10 8 6 4 2

I don't hold back
in this one

these pages hold
my darkest traumas

please proceed
with extra
caution

Xxoo

contains references to: eating disorders,
emotional abuse, exploitation, homophobia,
pedophilia, religion, sexual violence

Reflecting

Respiro profundo
  máscara puesta

  saludo con una sonrisa
para que duden la sospecha

  no quiero preguntas
no me gustan
  me asustan

  respondo con mentiras
para que no digan
la verdad
  que todos miran

la verdad
  que estoy escondiendo
muy adentro

    – Yo soy el camaleón

– I am the chameleon

deep inside
that i'm hiding
the truth

that everyone sees
the truth
so they don't say
i respond with lies

they scare me
i don't like them
i don't want questions

so they doubt the suspicion
i greet with a smile

mask on
I take a deep breath

I was a little boy

playing with my prima's barbies
secretly inside her closet
and of course
   always
with the door closed

i snuck around with her
doing things we knew
  we weren't allowed to

like when she did my makeup
we ran into the bedroom
locked the door
hid behind the bed
on the floor
while our entire family
was outside grilling
she brushed glitter blush
on my cheeks
as we sat there silently
  innocently

  half happy
i felt the most myself
but also anxious
  filled with fear of getting caught
doing things that i should not
  things that are only for girls
things that would make me the one thing
my family couldn't say out loud
  what wouldn't make them proud

this was only the beginning
  of my hiding
before i even knew
what i was hiding

   – Welcome to the closet

I manipulated myself

into believing
i was the version
   the church made me

every time
the real me
would rise
   i'd rebuke it

mentally,
and secretly
pray the prayer
i memorized
from repeating it
   so many times

until i was satisfied
   until my ocd
was convinced
i wasn't going into the abyss
   of hell
the home of the devil
the one who cursed me
   with my homosexuality

this is what the church
   instilled in me

   – Trauma is what they gave me

Pray it away

they say
  as if i haven't tried

you have to pray harder, longer
  and truly want it to go away he said
as if he knows what it's like
to be on your knees
with your fingers interlocked
in front of your heart
at the steps of the altar
every sunday night
crying, pleading, praying to god
to take away a special piece
  a gift that he blessed you with

i was created
  in the image of god
the bible says
  his word is the truth
i've heard pastors scream
  since i was in my mother's womb
that's why it hasn't changed
  why i still feel the same

i've tried and tried and tried
again and again and again
  and it doesn't go away

you don't pray to god
  to take back blessings he gave

so don't tell me i can pray it away
  if you were in my shoes
you'd know that isn't true

  – *Soy gay papa*

It's drilled in my head

the look on your face
when i said
  me gustan los hombres

you closed your eyes
as your face clenched
for dear life

your fingertips curled
into your palms
and you squeezed

as if to relieve
the physical pain
my four innocent words
brought to your heart

  – Soy gay mama

I asked god
   to take back
what he did

   to change me

i didn't want to be
   who he made me

i wanted to be
what the church
wanted to see

i tried to be
   i couldn't be

       – *It wasn't me*

Remember the time

we went out at night
  with a few friends
a rooftop bar
pothos vines wrapped around the pillars

shared a bottle of cider
  along with some laughs

as we walked out
  you turned to me and said *i'm gonna use the restroom*
i responded *do you want to wait till we get to my apartment?*
you mischievously said *or you can come with me?*
i immediately knew what you wanted to do
so of course
  i followed behind you

we entered the restroom
  and bolted straight to the biggest stall
we took turns pushing each other up against the wall
  as we kissed fiercely
  and our hands went to town on each other's bodies

i lived for that adrenaline rush
  filled with so much passion
those few seconds
  were nothing but magic

all the times you initiated
  all i did was reciprocate it

    – Remember when you wanted me?

You expressed to me several times
how much you wished
i wasn't a virgin

but you didn't
want to be
the one
to take it

     – Did your two fingers satisfy your craving?

I went numb

you went to the bathroom
to clean yourself up
you stood in the shower
as the water ran through your hair

i stayed in your bed
as the past few minutes ran through my head
while you scrubbed my essence off your skin
i lay naked
staring at the ceiling
processing what i had just done

i gave it away
just like that
it was gone

the thing i promised to keep
until i had a wedding ring
was no longer a reality

it happened
it's done
it was with you

i learned what sexual intimacy was supposed to feel like
how i was supposed to feel
on the inside

– My first time with a boy

I lit up

when you texted me
  can i pick you up?

of course i said *yes*
then off to dinner we went
we decided on mexican
  it wasn't authentic

back in the parking lot
i was in your passenger seat
you put your hand on my headrest
  looked at me
our eyes connected
the tension thickened
i predicted your next move
i was right
  you were ready for dessert

  so you leaned in
for a taste of my sweet lips
but i stopped you and said
  there's too many people around
so you turned the car on
  reversed
and took me on a beautiful course

we stopped in an empty lot
on top of a hill
  all we could see
were the sparkling lights of the city

we continued where we left off
  and enjoyed our favorite dessert

  – Licked the plate clean

Your level of experience
  was far beyond my reach

  still
i jumped in
ready to learn
  all of your techniques

  hoping to catch up
and in return
  teach you
a few things

– *How many before me?*

Your hand
  around my neck

my head hangs
off the edge
  of my bed

you choke me
  for pleasure
as i lie there
  gasping
for air

i thought
i was supposed to
  enjoy this

but all it brought me
  was pain
and confusion

but
  i never
refused

i let you do
whatever it took
  for you
to get off
  with me

     – *Get off of me*

We weren't lovers
  we weren't friends

we were in the middle
  on opposite ends

playing tug-of-war
  with my heart
hoping i didn't fall apart
while you tried to pull me to your side
so we could keep having our fun
  but also your freedom

i fought with every ounce of me
to get you on my side
but no matter how hard i tried
you didn't give up
you stood strong
  knowing what you want

i realized this war would never end
  so i let go

and settled with being
  just friends

    – Is something better than nothing?

A night out on the town

at the pub down the street
you took me to go meet
    the new boy in your life

we walked through the front entrance
handed the bouncer our IDs
i followed behind you
as you went to go see
where your new boy toy could be

you found him and immediately
    smiled
this was hard to watch
and as an automatic response
i joined in on the fun
    teeth and all

he was behind the bar
with a cocktail shaker in his hands
vigorously mixing the liquored potion
as his eyes magnetized to yours
    i watched this in slow motion

after pouring a few more drinks
he walked over to us
said his hellos
    i hugged him
and told him how great it was
to finally meet him
    of course i was lying
this was the one thing i was dreading

    he reciprocated my performance
i followed up with another generic phrase
    i've heard so much about you
this part was true
    although i wished it wasn't

i kept the performance going
as the small talk kept escalating
until it was finally time for him to return
to the drunken patrons wanting more

we found an empty table
grabbed a seat
   and enjoyed the cocktails he made
per his specialty

i tried to stay present in our conversation
but the only thing i could do
was picture how this boy got to touch you
   in all the ways i no longer do

and how much pain
he'd soon go through
   because of you

   – First time meeting him, last time seeing him

I know it felt different to you

   i wish it felt that way to me too
but no matter how many therapy sessions
and church services i attended

i couldn't shake the sensation inside
   i couldn't stop the butterflies
i couldn't make my mind be satisfied

with having just a friendly relationship again
   it always craved more
it always wished you would take it a step further
   like you did before

when will my body stop reacting to your touch?
   when will i feel nothing
when we hug?

    – From romantic to platonic

Eyes open

good morning
  i'm not hungry
cup of coffee
waiting for me
bathroom break
brew another cup
  i'm not hungry
  i'll wait

time to go to class
over one hundred degrees trapped in a room
dozens of bodies breathe and move

hip dips
sweat drips
burpees
my heart beats rapidly
  water has zero calories
big sips
  it'll flush everything out of me

i can't wait to get home to pee
and look in the mirror to see
if my stomach is flatter
than it was in the morning

  i'm still not hungry

cold shower
for shock therapy
protein shake
packed with all the vitamins
first meal of the day

let's get to work
  i'll eat after
many hours later

i'm so tired

too exhausted to cook something
let's go with the easiest option
grab something frozen
throw it on the stovetop

serve it
eat it
but
  don't finish it

the less i eat
the happier my mind will be
it's not about what my body needs
it's all about doing what i need
for my mind to be at ease

  i'm full
once i reach the limit
of spoonfuls
i set for myself
the second i sit down

i reach the perfect even count
i throw the rest away
time to relax
let's unwind
bring out the weed

i deserve something sweet
let's grab a treat

  i barely ate anything today
  i have extra calories to spend
  it's totally worth a binge
    i earned this

i chew away

convincing myself it's worth the taste
as i calculate
   how many calories

i'll continue to count
till i fall asleep
it's the first thing
i think about
every morning

   – Counting my calories

I have a photo shoot

  i hate modeling
i feel so awkward
and uncomfortable
  i don't know what to do with my body

the weeks leading up to a shoot
  anxiety walks me through

i starve myself
at least
  72 hours before
my call time

  48 hours before
i start swallowing pills
to rid me of all the water
hydrating my body

only an apple
  24 hours before
maybe a smoothie
  if i've exercised enough
and can afford
  the extra calories

i step on the scale
multiple times a day
  but only after
the toilet receives
as much as i can get out of me

i'll do whatever it takes
to get the number by my feet
down to the number
my brain tells me
will make me
  happy

i have no energy left to give
  i'm tired before i even begin

i stare into the camera lens
and smile real big
  it's easy for me to pretend

but at least i look good

i dread photo shoots
  i'm hungry

        – I need food

Food

what a blessing
until
all i can think about is
how many calories?

the anxiety hits me
the moment the plate
is in front of me

bullets through my chest
  i can't take full breaths

i'm scared
of gaining weight
  i must remain skinny

i can't work out too much
i can't have muscles
if i'm playing a kid
  on tv

i must stick
to the look
that will get me
  booked

        – I must remain skinny

Dance mannequin

i stand frozen
  multitasking

i have to coordinate my feet
with the rhythm of the costume ladies
  so the tall socks and boots can go on me

but also coordinate my hands
to lift up my shirt
so i can dance with the wire of the microphone
  as the sound guy straps it around me

as this is happening
the focus and energy i have remaining
goes to the director
as i listen to my new directions
  carefully

we only have seconds until the next take
but there stands hair and makeup
waiting their turn to touch up
  another part of me

hopefully there's a second to spare
so i can take a deep breath
before i have to do it
  all over again

  – *Action*

Realizing

The church
believes
   the only way
to heaven
is through the doors
  man created

    – Religion

They'll tell you

god bless you
  i'm praying for you

  right after their eyes
travel from your head
to your toes
then slowly
make their way back
  to your eyes

where they meet you
  with a fake smize

        – *The great demise*

You nod along like sheep

thinking you're better than everyone
because you clap along
know all the songs
attend service every week
the loudest one to scream
   amen
when the pastor is preaching

thirty-two inches of virgin hair
hanging down the back of chairs
   some hidden under bobby-pinned veils

they tell you what to wear
and how short your skirt can be
   they make you feel like a whore
if it's above the knee

women can't wear pants
   because they were created for men
they can't wear pants
because it's too suggestive
   so instead
they wear the tightest skirt in their closet
   but don't worry
at least their knees aren't showing
   you won't have anything to lust over

   jesus wore a dress back in the day
but if you're a boy today
   don't even think about it
unless you want to be taken into a room
   to rebuke
all the demons stuck inside
   telling you lies

don't you dare dye your hair
   or add color to your lips

you can't wear that
  it accentuates your hips

i better not see you next sunday with those nails
you look like a clown with that blush
wipe that mascara
  off

girls can't get haircuts
  boys must get buzz cuts

  don't even think about wearing any kind of jewelry
unless it's a watch
  then it's not a sin
even if it no longer ticks
  even if you check the time on your phone instead?

    – Let's go to church, they said

You tricked me

i was naive
  you were fifty years older than me

you groomed me
gave me toys
all the things a little boy could ever want
  to gain my trust
what better place to do this than
  god's home
which they say is the safest place you could be
  the most holy

you told me you were going to gift me
  clothing
but you needed to know my size
so you grabbed my hand
and took me to the darkest place in church
  the place nobody would go

outside
across the property
  behind the sunday school classrooms
by the tree
no lights
  it was hard to see

you grabbed my tiny shoulders
spun me around
telling me in spanish
  you were checking my pant size

one hand held your flip phone
  illuminating the scene
as you lifted up the back of my shirt
your other hand peeled back my pants
  you took pictures

i felt your old
   disgusting
swollen and crusty
fingers go down my pants
   beneath my underwear

your fingers took turns
sliding in and out of
   a place only my mother would touch
to wipe me clean

   – *Never got the clothing*

I suppress
what's going on inside
   and perform
my memorized actions and lines

afraid they'll see
the real me
hiding inside the person
i'm pretending to be
   the person i so badly wish i could be
for their comfort
and worst of all
for their approval
to decide if i'm holy enough
   worthy enough
of receiving god's love
and earning a spot
   in his kingdom

   i thought god's love was unconditional?
but then they'll say
   god loves the sinner but hates the sin
as if i'm able to rewire my brain
to lust only for
   a female's body parts

they also said
not to trust your heart
because it can lie
follow the bible
   it's the book of life

they program you to think
   instead of feel
they tell you how to think
and what to feel

      – Was it help or control?

They'll make you feel
like you don't belong
   like you're so far gone

they'll tell you they're concerned
   for your soul
they'll make you believe
you're lost and need their help
   to find home

even though
   god is everywhere

you must attend
   every service
and don't forget to
   bring a friend

sometimes raising funds
   comes before saving souls
worship for a few minutes
spend the next thirty
   talking about money

meanwhile some people in the congregation
   needed a ride to receive god's message
some of them came straight from work
   most of them are immigrants

funds are collected
   but most of the time
don't reach the expectation

what happens after?
   no one knows
it's never talked about again
   until there's a new project

   they don't care to understand

the church's demographic
   or the challenges they're facing

i think jesus would be disappointed
   to see quantity over quality

and transforming into the churches they preach against
   the ones where you're allowed to wear
jeans and earrings

church was never supposed to be a business
   it was never supposed to be for profit

people are supposed to give the amount
   god puts in your heart
is what they say

   but then whine about
not reaching the amount
   they wanted
who is this supposed to be benefiting?

numbers don't lie
   but churches certainly know
how to beat around
   that bush

   – Glory or gore?

The judgment you receive

the moment you step foot
   onto the property
hits deep

it's even more painful
and damaging
coming from people
claiming to be
family

once you decide to leave
they stop asking how you're doing
   talk about community

they'll be your best friend
   as long as
you're paying your ten percent

shop at the same stores
laugh at the same jokes
aim for the same goals

   don't forget to grab your mask
before you walk out the door
   make sure you change the tunes
to worship music
at least a mile before
you reach the white-painted
   metal gates of the church

this is what you call control
   this is a cult's ultimate goal

   – *Copycats*

I feel guilty
  for feeling happy

while doing the things
i used to pray
to god
to keep
away

– *Trauma*

Accepting and supporting

is
not
the
same
thing

– *Ask questions, learn the difference*

Sometimes
  i miss where i came from

i travel back to console
  the ache in my soul

but as soon as i arrive
i revert to an old version of me
a version i'm scared of
  the version i ran away from

i tried so hard to leave it behind
  but every time i return
it's at the front door
waiting for me
  anxiously

the switch turns on automatically
  second nature takes control of me
i become the version
  my mom and dad are most comfortable seeing

they're cheerful their baby boy is home
as am i
  with camouflaged resentment inside

we keep the conversations superficial
  this i'm used to
they only know a version of me
i made up to keep them
  happy

i wonder how much longer i can keep this up
  i wonder when i'll finally
    erupt

    – Viva Las Vegas

It's not all
   fun and games

it messes
  with your brain

it makes you question
if it's really
worth it

   – *Fame*

I used to think success meant living off your dreams

i was born with a special seed
grew up searching for the perfect soil
found it in a town called
  hollywood

 i left everything i knew
with the ones who encouraged me to follow my dreams
  and become who i'm destined to

i took my special seed and followed the instructions
  carefully
planted it with the love pouring out of me
  i sat back patiently
as i was told

waiting for it to burst into the garden
the grown humans promised it would become
  but only if i let them tell me when and how much to pour
i bought the plan they sold
  since it's worked for them many times before

i collected the fruits of my labor
  but only after the grown humans collected their share
whatever was left i used meticulously to feed me
but it only satisfied my reality
  my soul was still starving

   – Reap what you sow

They need you to depend on them
   so they can survive

they see the power in you
   it's more than they can produce
so they trick you
   to feed off you

they convince you
   they're right behind you
on the ladder to your dreams
and all the success
you spend every day fantasizing

they make you believe
it's within arm's reach
   if you just follow their lead

   but in reality
the ladder i was climbing
was designed by the one
   right behind me

this is the same equation
   all cults use

i wanted them
   they needed me

these are
   close enemies

   – *The entertainment industry*

Night
makes me think
of you

it was the only time
   you wanted me

   – When no one else could see

I was so green

thinking we could be
  something

why did i assume
the things we did
would lead to
you and me together
  committed forever?

i never even considered
such a thing as
  temporary love
or doing those things
  just for fun

    – My first

I confused
your lust
for love

   – Whose fault is that?

I'd beat myself up

  mentally
every time a memory
  of us
came to me

i'd tell myself it's a sign
  that i'm still not fully healed

  but after therapy
i realized a memory
doesn't have to be a bad thing

i can't train my brain
to forget every single thing
that happened between
you and me

  but i can teach it
to make peace
with history

and smile
  at the good
memories

      – *Outshine*

Quiero verte en tus ojos
  y sentir tu cuerpo

por lo mientras que escalamos
al lugar que siempre
  buscamos
un lugar que siempre
  exanamos

agarrame la mano
  yo te llevo
a un lugar nuevo

pero para llegar
  juntos
tenemos que dejar
el miedo

todo lo que tenemos
y queremos
  es este momento

  – *Vamos al cielo*

I want to look you in the eyes
and feel your body

as we climb
to the place we always
search for
a place we always
yearn for

grab my hand
i'll take you
to a new place

but to arrive
together
we must leave
the fear behind

all we have
and want
is this moment

– *Let's go to heaven*

Responding

I attended
the best
   acting program
to ever exist
on planet earth

   the church

they taught me
   how to pretend
and transform myself
into one of them

i didn't even know
i was acting
   it was method

      – I want to thank the academy

I was baptized

in the name of jesus christ
for forgiveness of my sins
  at the age of fifteen

i was told
  i would gain salvation in return
i was told
  i would be reborn
if i was submerged
under lukewarm water
  by the pastor

i believed it
  why wouldn't i
it was what i was taught since birth
it was my golden ticket into heaven
it was the only way to secure my spot next to god

i was hoping it would be the missing piece
that god needed to deliver me
  from my homosexuality

i thought i would finally receive
what the church promised me
  true love
from the creator of all things
  but i was wrong
instead it made me go further down the path
  god never wanted me to step foot on
the path that led me to self-destruction

  the church held my hand
as i walked down this path
once i reached my destination
  they let go
and let me suffer in my rock bottom
  alone

thank god they did
  so i could finally wake up
from the nightmare that is church
and follow the light that has always lived inside
that the church tried to dim
and make me believe
  wasn't for me

the light that led me down the path of healing
where i found peace and the greatest love of all
  better than the love religion tried to sell me

the love i paid ten percent of my income for
the love they twist and manipulate
to gain the evilest thing
  control
and of course the root of it all
  money

the evilest
  because they put god in the middle

they pray for the broken
  as they prey on the broken

what better people to manipulate
than those who are willing to do anything
  for salvation
from a life made out to be so corrupted

  they take advantage
transform them into followers of religion
  instead of teaching how to tap into
the source of all existence
and follow the unique reason
god gave us this
  human experience

  –Awakening

I harbor resentment
   towards the church

   not a single drop of it
towards god
or the temple itself
not even the classrooms
where i grew up learning
then eventually
teaching

every drop of my resentment
   belongs to the congregation
the people who make up the church
the ones who attend
   and especially the ones who run it

the people who walk up and down the rows
believing they are doing god's work
   by condemning others
for being who god created them to be
for being true to themselves
   and not pretending

   i hope one day they realize
they were wrong about all the things
they brainwashed me to believe

i thank god every day
   that i'm free
and that i survived
   to tell my story

        – *I hope they make it out*

I'm learning to feel

  i want to stop thinking so much
i want to stop judging
  each thought

i want to stop intellectualizing my emotions
  i just want to feel them
not have to convince myself
  i'm a good human

i'm learning how to feel my body
for the first time
  without my brain interrupting
reminding me of the memories
it associates with pain
all i get out of this
  is frustration

  i'm learning to unlearn all things religion
i'm learning to lean into the deepest parts of me
where the magic came from
but in order to use it
  i must illuminate all the dark
shine the light so my brain can see
it doesn't have to fight against anything

i'm learning to help my brain
  amplify my source

  my soul
will live forever
  my brain
is only for this lifetime

    – *Learning to work together*

I already have
   everything
i want and need

it all lives
   inside of me

     – Breathe

Only when
i accept
the reality
of the lessons
and learn to
smile at them
will i be able to
reap the benefits
of being
   divinely human

   –Peace

To simply be
is this life's
  biggest blessing

the one thing
we all desire
  but only some
have the courage
to fight for

those who do
  with love
receive what the universe
wants them to see

    – Love is free

I found a face that i like
and a vibe that matches mine

only been with you
    two nights
and i can already tell
there will be
    many more times

rock our hips
kiss your lips
make me feel
    like i can trust again

face down
back bent
make it easy
    to fall in love again

you press my magic button
    sends me to another dimension

you know just what i like
    more than i do

your hands work my body
    more than mine could

    you're an escape
i want to be trapped in

     – You make me feel more than human

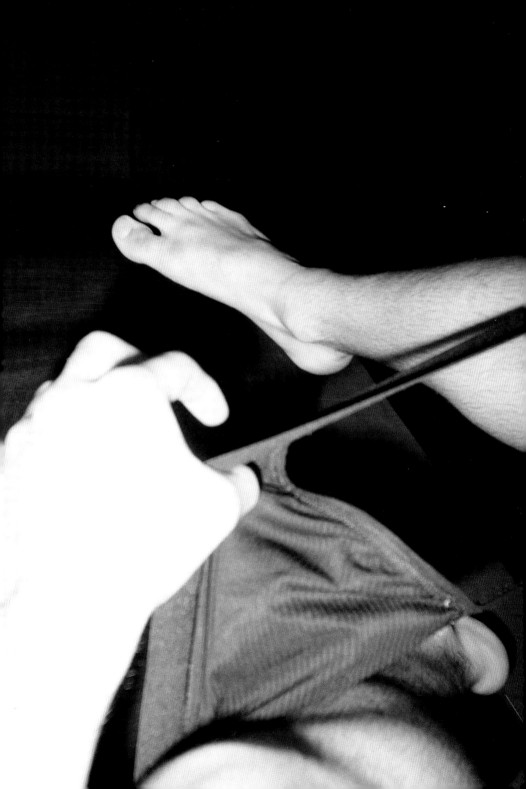

Hands on your knees
my head in between
   i please your needs
while on my knees

hands on my knees
your head in between
   you please my needs
while on your knees

   – *We take turns*

I gave it all
  lived and learned

i hit a wall
  watched it burn

reflected and accepted
  i let it all go
starting fresh
i'll do it all again
  but on my own

in this rebirth
  my art will hold
the light
once obscured

  my light
i do not control

i can simply
  watch it glow

and enjoy
  the growth
that comes from
  the hard work
only i can put forth

    – Independent

The more i grow

  the more i learn
about all the battles
tied to my soul

some from childhood
  some by nature
some to be fought
  others to accept
will never be gone

some treated
with many
  therapy sessions
others treated
  with medicine

some with natural substances
  others with pharmaceutical ones

all these battles
have already been
  won

just me trying
  every day
is enough

    – They do not define me

My heart is pure
   with good intention
there is no reason to question

as long as i'm following
   what's calling me
i know i'm fulfilling
   god's purpose for me

   i do not take
anything
   i choose only to receive
what the universe has
   for me

      –I'm ready

Lo aprendi de ti

la fortaleza para seguir
la paciencia para no rendir
la sabiduría para entender
la pasión para creer
　y determinación para mejor

más que nada
　aprendí a amar
incondicional

gracias por
aprender y crecer
　conmigo

　los amo
y estoy tan agradecido

　　– Mama y Papa

I learned it from you

the strength to continue
the patience to not give up
the wisdom to understand
the passion to believe
and determination for better

more than anything
i learned to love
unconditionally

thank you for
learning and growing
with me

i love you
and i am so grateful

　　– Mom and Dad

I'm here to feel
  it's a part of this experience

my soul deserves it all
  the bliss and fulfillment
of shining the light
  the universe meticulously placed in me

my soul is whole
  as it is
it's only organs and emotions
that get damaged
from the pain they endure

  i can try
to run and hide
from the challenges
  until they eventually find me

or i can face the pain head-on
  and flourish
to arrive in the new reality
  god has for me

the angels are excited to see me enter
  but only if i'm willing to surrender
and be a part of this magical experience

  – *Let's just be human*

You are doing
all you can

and that is all
you can do

Te Amo,

Abraham Rodriguez

Xxoo

Abraham Rodriguez is an actor, poet, interior designer, and artist based in Los Angeles. As an actor, he is best known for his roles in the iconic reboot of *Saved by the Bell* and *Power Rangers Beast Morphers*, earning him a Kids Choice Award nomination for Favorite Male TV Star. Abraham made his feature film debut in the psychological thriller *Exposure*. He is the owner of *Casita Gigante*, a home decor brand inspired by his Mexican roots. Abraham uses poetry to showcase the beauty and intricacies of vulnerability from the human experience. He is the author of *Mixed Feelings* and *Reborn*.

credits

creative direction: Abraham Rodriguez

editing: Jessica Peirce

proofreading: Molly Ringle

photography: Abraham Rodriguez

cover design & illustrations: Andress Belk

interior design: Michelle Halket

spanish proofreading: Laura Monteverde DeWalt

publisher: Central Avenue Publishing

sales & distribution: Simon & Schuster